William Page Wood

A Vindication of the Law Prohibiting Marriage with a Deceased Wife's Sister

I. On Social Principles; II. On Scripture Principles

William Page Wood

A Vindication of the Law Prohibiting Marriage with a Deceased Wife's Sister
I. On Social Principles; II. On Scripture Principles

ISBN/EAN: 9783743418899

Manufactured in Europe, USA, Canada, Australia, Japa

Cover: Foto ©Suzi / pixelio.de

Manufactured and distributed by brebook publishing software
(www.brebook.com)

William Page Wood

A Vindication of the Law Prohibiting Marriage with a Deceased Wife's Sister

A VINDICATION

OF THE

LAW PROHIBITING MARRIAGE

WITH A

DECEASED WIFE'S SISTER.

RIVINGTONS .

London	..	..	..	..	..	..	*Waterloo Place*
Oxford		..	..	..	..	..	*High Street*
Cambridge	..	.:	..	..	..	..	*Trinity Street*

A VINDICATION

OF THE

LAW PROHIBITING MARRIAGE

WITH A

DECEASED WIFE'S SISTER:

I. ON SOCIAL PRINCIPLES;

II. ON SCRIPTURE PRINCIPLES:

In Two Letters,

ADDRESSED TO THE

DEAN OF WESTMINSTER

(NOW ARCHBISHOP OF DUBLIN),

CHAIRMAN OF THE MARRIAGE LAW DEFENCE ASSOCIATION.

By SIR WM. PAGE WOOD

(NOW LORD HATHERLEY).

RIVINGTONS,
London, Oxford, and Cambridge.
1869.

" It is good also not to try experiments in States except the necessity be urgent, or the utility evident ; and well to beware that it be the reformation that draweth on the change, and not the desire of change that pretendeth the reformation."

BACON'S ESSAYS.

LETTER I.

THE LAW VINDICATED ON SOCIAL PRINCIPLES.

Dear Mr. Dean,

On the 27th of February, 1850, I discharged a very painful duty by taking part in the debate on the Bill for enabling widowers to marry the sister of their deceased wife. I say a painful duty, for the very discussion of such a subject is, to my mind, most perilous to the best interests of society; for which opinion I shall, I hope, before I conclude, adduce sufficient reasons.

From the tone and temper evinced by some members of the House of Commons it was clear to me that I should damage the weight of the arguments I might adduce against the proposed measure, were I to lay any stress upon Scriptural denunciations against such a marriage. I rested, therefore, my argument solely on the comparatively low, yet firm, ground of social policy, contenting myself with a simple avowal of my own belief in the higher prin-

B

ciples on which the discussion might be based. I
had the satisfaction of convincing some who had
previously voted for the Bill, and whom I had the
pleasure of seeing in the same lobby as myself on
subsequent divisions; I have subsequently found
that several earnest believers in Scripture (such,
indeed, were the gentlemen I have referred to)
have, on considerations of social policy, been led to
abandon the notion that any alteration of our long
settled law is desirable, though yet unconvinced of
the Scriptural prohibition of the marriages in
question.

I have no longer the opportunity of orally im-
pressing my views on the Legislature, but I cannot
conscientiously remain silent on a question which
involves a moral and social revolution. I have
laboured, and will, whilst health and life remain,
labour to the utmost of my power, to avert a great
national calamity. The affair assumed a far more
menacing aspect, when a Bill similar to that proposed in 1850 had, in 1859, not only passed the
House of Commons, but had been rejected by a majority of 10 only in the House of Lords. You, sir,
were among the first to arouse us to associated
action in opposing the systematic efforts of an
anonymous association, making up by wealth for
what it wanted otherwise in weight, to unsettle our
homes and destroy the fraternal relationship now
existing between brother and sister in law. I
gladly united myself to the Marriage Law Defence

Association, over which you preside, and on the 1st February, 1860, I was requested to move the first resolution at a public meeting convened by that Society at Willis's Rooms. The meeting was a remarkable one in many ways. Not only was the room crowded, but, although it was held during the business hours of the day, it was attended by a majority of men as compared with women, and by a majority of laymen as compared with clergymen. I was then asked to print a correct copy of the speech, and did my best, with the assistance of the short-hand writer's notes, to reproduce my arguments. But I have continued to observe such remarkable ignorance of the former and existing state of our law upon the subject, such persevering misrepresentation (I will not call it wilful) of the effect of Lord Lyndhurst's Act of 1835, such blindness to the inevitable, and not remote, consequences of breaking down the barriers, that from the first existence of our nation have separated incestuous from lawful marriages, that I am not content to let another Session of Parliament pass without doing my best to make the law known, so that its misrepresentation shall no longer be excusable, and without pointing out the necessary consequences of its alteration. The Lord Chancellor, some very eminent retired Judges, and other distinguished members of my own profession, are to be found enrolled as members of our Association, and though they will not be responsible

for any errors of law on my part, yet it is a
satisfaction to me to know that I assert no legal propositions, but those which I can venture to submit
even to their scrutiny. I have, however, divided the
substance of my argument into two letters, because
I wish carefully to separate the ordinary, though
cogent, moral and social reasons for objecting to an
alteration of the law, from those that are founded
on a belief in Revelation. I shall in this my first
letter address myself to those who either altogether
reject Scriptural authority on the subject, or deny
that it can be cited in opposition to the marriage in
question. If the Bible had never existed, the arguments contained in this letter would lose no weight.
In my second letter I shall give my reasons for
believing that the Word of God has spoken autho-
ritatively on the subject.

Some of the supporters of the proposed change
have, with an unfairness which always implies con-
scious weakness in the advocate, adopted the vulgar
course of nicknaming their opponents. "The opposition to the 'Wife's Sister's Marriage Bill' (it has
been said) is a High Church, or Puseyite opposition." This assertion is simply ridiculous in face
of the facts. Neither the Archbishop of Canterbury
amongst our prelates, nor the Earl of Shaftesbury
amongst our distinguished religious laity, nor the
"Record" amongst religious journals, nor the established Kirk in Scotland, has ever been suspected
of ultra High Church tendencies, yet all support the

views of the Marriage Law Defence Association.
Our opponents have printed and paraded the Scriptural expositions of Cardinal Wiseman, and of Jewish
Talmudists (the upholders of tradition amongst the
Jews), as favourable to their views, and they shall
enjoy their advocacy without any suspicion on my
part of a tendency on theirs to Popery or Judaism.
I hope they will not accuse me of Puritanism if, in
my second letter, I should refer to the opinion of
the "Assembly of Divines," or of Puseyism because
I may borrow an argument from some of the learned
writings of Dr. Pusey. Let the controversy be
carried on, at least as between gentlemen, and
" God defend the right."

Whilst I was in the House of Commons the
question was not treated as a party one, either
religiously or politically. Two of the best speeches
that I heard on our side were delivered by the late
Mr. Sheil, and by Mr. Roebuck, respectively. I
saw, however, with regret, symptoms in 1859 of a
political and party spirit in the debates. I mention
this because I think the principles which are at
issue lie far deeper than the very superficial lines
that now divide political parties in our country.

I will first endeavour to state exactly our existing law,—the length of time during which it has
prevailed,—and the necessary social consequences
of its prevalence. We shall thus alone acquire an
adequate appreciation of the onus necessarily cast
on those who attempt its alteration.

The following propositions will be found to be beyond dispute.

I. That the Law of England, both Ecclesiastical and Civil, has from the first constitution of our monarchy treated marriage with a wife's sister as an incestuous marriage, and has never, down to the present day, made any distinction whatever between such a marriage, and a marriage with a man's own sister or even mother.

II. That by the same Law, and from the same time, *all* incestuous marriages have been wholly void, and not merely voidable, but the Ecclesiastical Courts (which alone had jurisdiction in all matters of marriage) were not allowed to declare a marriage void after the decease of either husband or wife, being prevented by prohibition from the Civil Courts from so doing, though they were allowed to punish the surviving parent for incest. Consequently a child born of a man's own sister after a ceremony of marriage between the parents, could not, after the death of either parent, be pronounced to be illegitimate; and the rule as to the offspring of the marriage with a man's own sister was exactly the same.

III. That Lord Lyndhurst's Act of 1835 did not make any difference of degree between incestuous marriages, and the whole of that Act applies exactly in the same manner to a marriage with a man's own sister as to a marriage with a wife's sister.

IV. That Lord Lyndhurst's Act did not declare any then existing incestuous marriage to be good, but prevented any suit in the Ecclesiastical Court for declaring void such existing marriage, whether the parents were living or not; but as to any future incestuous marriage, declared it void, and so allowed it to be set aside after the death of the parents.

Fortunately, I am enabled thus to state the law without fear of contradiction, on the authority of the very recent case of Fenton v. Livingstone, decided by the House of Lords in July, 1859, and reported in the "Jurist" of the 3rd December, 1859.

Our opponents frequently represent the Act of 1835, commonly called Lord Lyndhurst's Act, as that which first invalidated the marriages in question, saying, that till then they were only voidable[1]. I stated in the House of Commons ten years ago that this was a gross mistake, that such marriages were absolutely invalid at all times by our law, and from the time of Henry VIII. had been so dealt with by statute. The mistake arose in the manner described by Lord Brougham in moving the judgment of the House of Lords in Fenton v. Livingstone. There a Scot domiciled in England, had in the year 1808 (long before Lord Lyndhurst's Act)

---

[1] I observed that two of our more respectable papers, the "Globe" and "Daily News," in commenting on the proceedings at Willis's Rooms, fell into this common blunder, and much of their reasoning was built on this false assumption.

married his deceased wife's sister and had by her a
son. This marriage was *not declared* void during
the lifetime of those who had contracted it, and
could not, owing to the peculiarity of the jurisdiction of our Ecclesiastical Court, to which I have
referred, be *declared* void afterwards, so that a
child could not, *in England*, be afterwards *proved* to
be illegitimate. It was therefore contended that the
marriage was a valid marriage, and that the child
could inherit land in Scotland; but Lords Brougham,
Cranworth, Wensleydale, and Chelmsford, were
unanimously of opinion that the marriage was
illegal and invalid by English law from the first,
and that the child could not inherit the property.
Lord Brougham thus clearly states the law:—

" It (viz. the marriage) was clearly illegal by the
law of England. That law treated it as incestuous
by the Rules of the Ecclesiastical Court, which
alone has cognizance of this objection to a marriage.
It could not be questioned except during the lives
of husband and wife; but it was illegal, and if
questioned while both parties were alive, it must
have been declared void *ab initio*. And why?
Because it was contrary to law. The circumstance
of one party to it having died before the dispute
arose, and before it was questioned, did not make
the marriage legal, though it precluded the possibility of setting it aside. And the son was issue
not of a lawful marriage, but of a marriage which
could not be questioned with effect, according to

the rules of the Ecclesiastical Court (that Court alone having jurisdiction upon the question), by the rules which govern the temporal Courts. But they hold the same principles on this subject as the Ecclesiastical, and would act upon them, if they could entertain the question."

I have, however, given the clear opinions of the several learned lords upon these points more fully in the Appendix. They will repay the perusal. It is amusing to observe that the Rev. Mr. Bacon, who has addressed a letter to the Bishop of Lichfield on the subject, in which he appears to be in a very great passion with myself for my speech at Willis's Rooms, complains that I assert such marriages were always void by the law of England, and then adds these words: " It is a most remarkable thing that the Vice-Chancellor, to prove it not virtually permitted, cites the case of a Scotch gentleman married in England having property in Scotland, in which it was decreed a child of such marriage could not inherit. Why is dust thus thrown in the eyes ? We are speaking of England, not of Scotland. Here many properties are inherited under such marriages." If this gentleman will only take the trouble to read the case, or even the Appendix to this letter, he will see the point wholly turned on English law, and not on Scotch law. If the marriage had been good by the law of England, the child would have inherited the land in Scotland. I do not think it necessary to answer the reverend gentleman's accusations of "partial views of evidence," "incorrectness of statement," "impotence of argument," further than by asking, "Tantæne animis cœlestibus iræ ?"

The same authority completely settled another point raised by the supporters of a change in the law. They have repeatedly stated, and unhappily a so-called *Society* for altering the law (which is, however, strictly anonymous, and I know not whether it consists of more than one individual) has frequently advertised that a marriage with a wife's sister contracted in any foreign country where it is not forbidden, will be valid in England. The advertisement stated a well-known decision of Lord Stowell, that a marriage lawfully contracted according to the law of the country where it is celebrated, is a valid marriage every where else. And they then added, "The Law of Denmark allows marriage with a deceased wife's sister." These advertisements, I am sorry to say, were continued, long after the decision in the Sussex Peerage case had established that to this general rule there was an exception, when the parties so marrying were disqualified by the positive law of their own country from intermarriage. The same point has now been expressly decided by Fenton *v.* Livingstone, and Lord Wensleydale lays down the law on this subject in a clear manner, as may be seen at length in the Appendix.

I fear many women have unfortunately been betrayed into these illegal marriages by the delusive advertisements I have referred to. In fact, Lord Lyndhurst's Act of 1835, in mercy to those who might be entrapped into marriages that might at any time (during the life only of either party, as the law then stood) be declared void at the caprice of the husband, or from the malice of an enemy, or on the real conscientious interference of friends, made them impossible.

The title of this Act of Lord Lyndhurst is no doubt misleading. It runs thus : " An Act to render certain Marriages valid, and to alter the law with respect to certain voidable Marriages." Now, the Act does not render (as it has often, through inadvertence, been asserted to do) any marriage within the prohibited degrees valid, but only says that the marriages which at the date of this Act had been solemnized within those degrees should not be questioned, although the husband and wife were both living. Sir Herbert Jenner refers to this in his judgment in Ray v. Sherwood Curtis, 193. He says, " The enacting part of the Act does not make these marriages to be good and valid to all intents and purposes, as might be supposed from the title of the Act ;" and he proceeds to state his opinion that the parties to such a marriage would still be punishable for incest in the Ecclesiastical Courts, though married before the Act. This, in fact, is the important distinction throughout. Before Lord Lyndhurst's Act, the

Ecclesiastical Court could not declare the marriage void after the death of either party, but it could punish the survivor for incest. And so it could in the case of parties whose marriages were prohibited from being declared void by Lord Lyndhurst's Act. When it is recollected that the Act would apply to marriage with a man's own sister, it will be seen to be right to leave the parties punishable.

Such then is our law, and such has it been at all times, the only modification being that which I have last mentioned.

Before the Reformation the Ecclesiastical Courts alone, and without restraint, determined what was a valid, and what was an invalid marriage. The Civil Courts adopted their decision as conclusive. This is wholly irrespective of the merits of such a state of law. I deal only with the facts at present. The Ecclesiastical Courts always held the marriage with the wife's sister to be invalid from the time when Christianity commenced in this island. True it is that when the corruptions of the Romish system prevailed, you could buy a papal dispensation from the law. But even this corrupt course never existed in practice here; and, indeed, the first known grant, any where, of a papal dispensation to marry a wife's sister was made, very shortly before the Reformation, to King John of Portugal by Alexander Borgia, who himself lay under the imputation of most disgraceful incest. The Church of Rome had indeed adopted a course which led to great abuse. They extended the prohibited degrees far beyond those contained in the 18th chapter of Leviticus, and then dispensed with the prohibition for a money payment. At the Reformation this abuse was corrected by the 32 Hen. VIII. c. 38, which enacted amongst other things, "That no reservation or prohibition, God's law except, shall trouble or impeach any marriage without the Levitical degrees." The Common Law Courts upon this statute determined, that the Levitical degrees were to be extended to all degrees of the same proximity, either by affinity or consanguinity, as those named in the 18th chapter of Leviticus (see the very interesting cases of Harrison v. Burwell, and Hill v. Good, in Chief Justice Vaughan's Reports, in the time of Charles II.), and that the case of the wife's sister was within the Levitical degree. At no time, up to the present hour, has any difference been made between that case and the case of a man's own mother or sister.

The time, then, during which the existing system of law prevailed dates at least from the conversion of Ethelbert in the sixth century. Observe, however, that in this branch of my argument I claim no additional sanction from its Christian origin, or from the Book of Leviticus ; I claim merely a right to rely on the fact of the long duration of the law, and on the fact of the habits of thought and life thereby engendered, to which I will now call attention.

The social consequences of such a state of law
were obviously these,—an habitual recognition of
the wife's sister as a near member of the husband's
own family, and a consequent freedom of intercourse, going far beyond that which is allowed between a husband and any woman with whom he
could, in case of his wife's predecease, be at liberty
to intermarry. I appeal to every one's experience
on this head. It is very well for our opponents,
as some have done, to assume a superior degree of
purity, and to ask whether there be not grossness
of conception at the very root of our objection to a
change of the law. I answer them by these other
questions. Do not married men exercise privileges
of familiarity in regard to their sisters-in-law,
which custom does not permit with regard to
women in general, although no doubt a pure mind
might be trusted equally in either case? Do
widowers and ladies with whom they are at liberty
to contract marriage reside alone and unmarried in
the same house? and do not widowers, without
scandal, so reside with their sisters-in-law [2]?

It is not because the majority of men are gross,
but because not only the majority, but all, are
weak, that all laws, whether of Heathens, Jews,
or Christians, have fenced round the inhabitants of

[2] See an interesting communication from an American
Clergyman in the Appendix to my second letter on the total
change of social relationship introduced by such a change of
the law as is now advocated.

our homes with certain prohibitions of marriages, as I shall presently show. The very terms, mother-in-law, brother-in-law, sister-in-law, indicate the ideas that (in our country at least) have grown up in men's minds under the sanction of laws coeval with our social organization as a state. But the proposed Bill will, in fact, if entertained, abolish all those relationships. Moreover, the law having once (rightly or wrongly) classed the mother-in-law and sister-in-law with the mother and sister, as persons with whom no marriage can be had, this association alone (wholly independently of *religious* belief) has generated a repugnance to such marriages, as being all equally open to *moral* objection. In this country, till very lately, and in Scotland to the present hour, this repugnance has been an all but universal feeling. It is, perhaps, though I will not now be sure, still universal as to the mother-in-law. The long acquiescence, indeed, in the law can only be accounted for by the habitual and universal recognition of its propriety.

Having now established—1st, That, contrary to repeated blundering assertions as to the effect of Lord Lyndhurst's Act, marriage with a deceased wife's sister has, from at least the sixth century, or for 1200 years, been as absolutely illegal and void in England as that with a man's own sister; and having commented on the necessary results produced by the prevalence of such a state of the law for such a period; I have thrown, I think, a heavy

burden of proof on those who desire a change, to
show that such a change would be beneficial.

I proceed to test their arguments for that purpose, without supposing the existence of any special
revelation of God's will upon the subject.

1. They say marriage itself is a social institution
highly to be favoured, and that where God is silent
man should not presume to restrict the liberty of
marriage.

I admit the inestimable value of marriage as a
social institution; and in this letter, for argument's
sake, I take as admitted the silence of God's law,
but I totally deny the consequence—that society
ought not to restrict the liberty of marriage except
with Divine sanction.

I say, as a matter of fact, that no civilized
society has ever existed that has not by law restricted the liberty of marriage, and certain bar-
barous tribes of India are no real exception. The
restriction has been applied to different degrees of
relationship, according to the different social habits
of the country, but no civilized nation has permitted
the marriage of father and daughter, or son and
mother. I believe the Apostle Paul was not (as a
matter of fact) in error when he asserted that none
of the Gentiles tolerated a marriage with a step-
mother, a case, be it observed, of affinity. It is
well known that an unhappy attachment of step-
mother to step-son, and the converse, have been
recorded, and poetically and historically exhibited

by heathen authors as instances of depraved affection.

I can take my stand then on social grounds, independently of revelation, in saying that human laws have in all ages restricted marriage. I say they have rightly done so. What, indeed, is marriage itself but a restriction of promiscuous intercourse? Is this right or wrong? To him who does not admit revelation the test must be—does it produce more or less happiness? I will not stop to argue this. No Englishman, at present at least, will uphold promiscuous intercourse, or even polygamy [3]. The home, the undivided affection of the wife, the children, not too numerous for the exercise of the affections, nor the offspring of so many mothers as to create family dissension, are felt to justify the restraint independently of higher motives. The restriction then of marriage itself, as was beautifully said by the Bishop of Oxford at the

[3] Mr. Bacon, in his pamphlet before referred to, commenting on an objection raised by the Bishop of Oxford, and insisted on also by myself, to the raising of such social questions as the present, says that such remarks savour of the Inquisition. He does not appear to have reflected on the possibility of good feeling extinguishing discussion on some subjects. I do not believe that the House of Commons would tolerate a debate on the lawfulness of marriage with a man's own sister, and they would stop it without recourse to the methods of the Inquisition. Mr. Bacon, I am sure, would not desire discussion on some of the subjects mooted by Anacharsis Clootz. I believe that much mischief has already arisen from attempts to withdraw one case from the well-defined list of prohibited marriages.

C

late meeting at Willis's Rooms, though in form a
prohibition, is in reality a blessing. It is a fence
round the home, and all that that word contains.
But the same foresight, human only if you will,
which has discountenanced promiscuous intercourse and polygamy, has guarded further human
weakness by saying, that when a married man or
woman is, from circumstances, in constant habits
of intercourse and necessary daily familiarity with
other women or men, there shall be a prohibition
of all thought of union; otherwise the familiarity
which now adds largely to our happiness will be
but a snare. All nations have, therefore, wisely
fenced all the inmates of the home, the mother,
the daughter, the sister, by such prohibitive regu-
lations, though you may assume them to have been
destitute of all revelation, traditional or written,
on the subject. Hence too, perhaps, the peculiarity
of the unions allowed in some Eastern nations,
where the brothers and sisters are kept separate
from infancy.

Now that the near relations of the wife should
be entitled to the *privilege* of this prohibition, for
so I regard it, is a natural step in civilization, and
will prevail more and more where the intercourse
becomes more familiar, as in all Christian countries
it has done. The Romans, the Greeks, and all
other civilized nations have therefore rightly restrained marriage as to the step-mother and certain
other relationships, though only by affinity.

2. The promoters of the change next aver, that at all events the particular restraint in question has become irksome in this country, has long since been so in Germany and in some states of America, and ought now to be abolished.

3. That the aunt is the natural substitute for the mother to her deceased sister's children.

4. That this last observation applies more especially to the poor, by whom the abolition of the whole law is, they say, accordingly more especially desired.

I will take these three arguments together. That there may be some people to whom this restraint, like all other restraints, may be irksome, of course I will not deny. The restraint of marriage itself is irksome to many. Whether impatience, on the part of some, of a law that for 1200 years has governed the domestic habits of every family in the kingdom, justifies its abolition, depends on the comparative degree of injury to be inflicted on the impatient few by its retention, or the, at present at least, acquiescent many by its abolition. Now to repeal the law necessarily involves the total abolition of the relationship of sister-in-law. There are only three possible ways in which a man can treat his wife's sister. Either their intimacy will be, as at present, in its degree and character—viz. the intimacy of a brother and sister, in which case the idea or desire of a marriage union will never present itself to a well-regulated mind; or it will be an intimacy as close, but of a totally different character, in which case it will be highly perilous to both; for what woman with whom a union by marriage is possible is ever allowed the degree of intimacy in question? or, lastly, the intimacy will cease, the wife's sister will be as any other woman. She may not any longer venture on the innocent familiarities of a sister, nor reside alone with an individual brother-in-law. The last is the best result that can occur from our relaxation of the law.

Great indeed will be the loss—great the misery to sisters-in-law—and in thousands of families the brother-in-law, on his part, loses an equal happiness; nay, the wife herself will have far less frequent intercourse with her own sister. If her husband now become a widower, he has all the world to choose a wife from, except only his sister-in-law and the other near relations of his wife. This last is the whole amount of the hardship of the existing law—for I really can give no weight to the argument that the aunt is the best substitute for a mother to his children. The argument is all the other way. She can act as such mother now, and live with him after his wife's decease for that purpose, and does so continually; but why must she marry him? Mr. Roebuck well observed, the aunt's fitness for taking charge of the children is not improved by her becoming their step-mother. Her having children of her own to compete with them is rather, if any thing, an impediment to her doing so; and why too is the husband's own sister thought incompetent to the office? If this change be made, it is only as a step-mother that you can ask a wife's sister to take care of your children, for she cannot reside as a single woman in your house, and you will lose the most delicate-minded aunts as guardians. You literally, therefore, defeat your alleged object [4]. It is too much to assume that the persons who have broken the law by making these alliances have been thinking of their children. Few men who marry a second time think so much of their children as of their own comfort in a second wife and family, though they may deceive themselves into a belief that their motive is pure benevolence to their offspring. But then again, the poor man wishes (it is said) for the change. Now I must protest against this often repeated, and as often disproved assumption. It can be demonstrated to be utterly

[4] In the extraordinary evidence collected on the inquiry into the existing state of the law by the professional exertions of the able firm of Crowder and Maynard, and laid before Her Majesty's Commissioners, there is, among the honourable exceptions to the general rule of first breaking the law and then finding fault with it, one case of a gentleman, who, in answer to question 919 as to what feeling restrained him from asking his sister-in-law to live in his house, says, "I should say it was partly from the feeling that it was a delicate position to place a young female in to whom I was attached." This unhappy and perverted attachment thus deprived him of the comfort that thousands enjoy.

untrue that there is any special prevalence of such illegal marriages, or any special wish for such, among the poor.

In the first place, the poor are usually the last persons to change old habits and ideas, and, therefore, little likely to think of marriages contrary to the accustomed course. In the next place, the poor marry so early that it rarely occurs that the widower finds a sister of his wife disengaged, unless she be herself a widow. Those who do not marry early are in service, and not likely to leave it for a poor brother-in-law's house, in order to take on them the care of a sister's family.

But I do not rest on conjecture as to this; I go to the evidence produced by those wealthy promoters of all the agitation on this subject, who retained the respectable firm of Crowder and Maynard to bring their case before the Royal Commission of 1847. That evidence alleged that there were 1648 cases of marriages either had, or *prevented* (as they stated) by Lord Lyndhurst's Act, within the prohibited degrees. These instances have been tabulated, and show 1608 to be in the upper and middle classes, and 40 only among labourers and mechanics. The ratio is literally infinitesimal, if we reflect on the comparative number of individuals constituting the classes themselves.

I myself instituted an inquiry amongst the poor of the parishes of St. Margaret and St. John, Westminster, which contain more than 60,000 inhabitants, 40,000 (at least) of the poorer class. I found one case only, and in that case the man was "looked down upon," as my witness ascertained, the general feeling being very strong against such a marriage. I stated this in the House of Commons, in 1850, and a City Missionary of the same district wrote to the "Times" to say I had made a misstatement, for he had found two more cases! This was the result of our several, and, I believe, together very complete researches.

You will find many witnesses before the Commissioners dealing in vague generalities about the number of the poor who wish to make such marriages. Every body well knows the worthlessness of such generalities. A Clergyman wrote to me, in 1850, and said he knew amongst the poor many such instances, and that I was quite mistaken. I answered, "Send me the exact number you know, with an assurance that the case is within *your own knowledge*, and I will state the facts in an appendix to my speech which I am printing." I received no answer.

And now, sir, I have really gone through every alleged ground for the change. Assume, if you will, 5000 instead of 1648 persons who have so married, or desire to marry, I should not admit this as a ground for altering the condition of every other family in the kingdom [5].

[5] The evidence before the Commissioners of Inquiry of 1847 was analyzed, and its utter worthlessness exposed, in a very able letter of Alexander Beresford Hope, Esq., to Sir Robert Harry Inglis, published by Ridgway in 1849, which every one

But I come to graver questions, and I venture to assert some positive propositions of my own :—

I. The breaking of a law by a large number of persons is no ground for its repeal.

II. The alleged fact that a law can be broken without the offenders losing caste (as it is termed), in such a delicate matter as that which is the subject of our inquiry, would not, if true, afford ground for its repeal.

III. The fact that the prohibition of the given description of union has for centuries been part only of a series of prohibitions of other unions, such as that of father and daughter, brother and sister, uncle and niece, which last union at present no one is bold enough to advocate, affords in itself a chief ground for not tampering with the feelings that have sprung up as to what is or is not an incestuous union.

IV. The desire for a relaxation of laws relating to intercourse between the sexes has occurred, historically, in times of general relaxation of the morals of the society where that desire is experienced.

V. The relaxation once commenced must necessarily lead to increased appetency for unions still left out of reach.

VI. The happiness of the many would by any

should peruse who wishes to give a serious thought to the subject before he aids by his vote so mischievous an alteration of our social system.

change of the law be sacrificed to the gratification of a morbid craving on the part of the few.

My first proposition will be probably conceded. The statistics of crime would otherwise furnish ground for the repeal of every law. If the statistics of unions deemed by all (at present) to be incestuous (such as brother and sister, uncle and niece), had been collected by Messrs. Crowder and Maynard, they would in the case of the poor, at least, have been found far more abundant than those of the marriages in question : one clergyman sent to our Society a statement that he had found in a large district but three cases of the marriages in question, and *ten* cases of brother and sister living together. This is no doubt owing to the wretched arrangements of the poor man's dwelling ; a subject to which every philanthropist should give his attention[6].

My second proposition is, that the alleged fact that persons do not lose by breaking the law affords no ground for its repeal, and it rests on this

---

[6] It is not, happily, a common occurrence for educated people in this country to talk so coolly of breaking the law as an anonymous Solicitor before the Commissioners, who in answer to question 874 says, "I had a communication with two or three Clergymen, and the expression of one in particular was, that it was neither inconsistent with the divine law nor any other law, because he *repudiated*, very much as many gentlemen have done, the late Act!" Pickpockets repudiate Acts of Parliament, but it is not usual for Clergymen or Solicitors to do so.

ground. They do not lose caste for many things which no moralist, however lax, would sanction. It is grossly immoral, I conceive, in the existing state of the law, for a man to induce a woman to place herself in such a position that a large proportion of society will withdraw themselves from her company, and that her children must be illegitimate. It is still more immoral if he commit perjury (as those married to a wife's sister by licence must have done), in order to make such an illegal marriage. If people think this *respectable*, what will they not think so ? Indeed, in the evidence I have before referred to, Mr. Thorburn, in answer to question 123, states the case of "a man of wealth who keeps his carriage, *and lives avowedly, in fact, with his deceased wife's sister*, whom he would gladly marry but for the uncertain state of the law. He is *much respected, and bears a high character as an excellent man and a good citizen; and though he is living in open concubinage, his neighbours sympathize with him, and in a manner excuse him, because of the restraint of an inexpedient law !*" If this witness had but recollected his Latin Grammar, he would have known a heathen's notion of a good citizen and moral man, even in Rome's degenerate days, to be of a far higher stamp of morality :

"Vir bonus est quis ?
Qui consulta patrûm, qui leges juraque servat."

It appears to me I can hardly say more to show

the worth of connivance by *respectable* people at law-breaking, as evidence of a propriety of altering the laws. Neither marriage effected by perjury, nor illicit concubinage with the deceased wife's sister, seem to shock such respectability. This, indeed, proves my fourth proposition and my second at once.

My third proposition depends on the simple operation of the law of association. There has hitherto been no distinction between the marriage in question and other prohibited marriages. The same law forbids a marriage with a man's own sister, or his aunt, or niece, and with his wife's sister. Lord Lyndhurst's (the most recent Act) draws no line of distinction whatever. If this case is to be an open question, why not necessarily all the others? In truth this circumstance, to some extent, has been pointed out, as I shall have occasion to show, by Lord John Russell in debate.

Fourthly, on the tendency of mankind in an age of relaxed morality to demand relaxations in marriage restrictions, I have, more than once, quoted the well-known case of the Emperor Claudius seeking for a bill to enable him to marry his own niece. Any one may read what Tacitus says of such a proof of degenerate morality. But the speech of the Emperor's satellite to the senate is worthy of again being cited : " Nova nobis in fratrum filias conjugia, sed aliis gentibus solemnia, nec ullâ lege prohibita, et sobrinarum, diu ignorata, tempore addito percrebuisse : *morem accommodari prout conducat*, et fore hoc quoque in his quæ mox usurpentur." I may paraphrase the argument thus : " Well, our people don't much like these marriages, our ancestors had prejudices on the subject, but look at Germany and America, they are very common there. Our manners must be adjusted to the spirit of the age. People will soon get used to it." Claudius married his niece, and she poisoned him !

But as to the relaxation of morals, let me point out an analogy pregnant with warning. Divorces had been almost unknown during the Roman republic, but had under the Emperors become rife. What do our own Divorce Courts show of the moral state of our people on the subject of marriage ? I was a member of the Divorce Commission. I do not regret our recommendation, that what has been conceded to the rich should be allowed to the poor. It is not the remedy I regret, I conceive divorce for adultery to be justified by God's law, but I am appalled at the extent of the disease. We are told to look at Germany and America on the wife's sister question. Now in Germany, and I believe in most of the states of America where these marriages are allowed, divorce is allowed almost at will. Our Commission resolved that nothing but adultery ought to afford a ground for divorce. Will any one cognizant of either American or German society tell you that morals are not there fearfully relaxed on the question of marriage ? I

insert in the Appendix to my second letter extracts
from an interesting letter of a clergyman of South
Carolina on the subject of these two nearly con-
nected questions, the selection of one of the prohibited degrees for relaxation, and the facility of
divorce. I have given the extracts fully and fairly,
whether they appear in any way to press for or
against my view. The whole result is to my mind
clear as to the result of the relaxation. In either
of those two countries the wife can scarcely invite
her sister-in-law to her home, without the possible
prospect of her immediate succession to her as its
mistress. At present in our country, even should
the law be altered, the sister-in-law could only
look forward to the reversion. True it is, that
nearly every country, that has relaxed the prohibition as to the wife's sister, has also relaxed the
law of divorce; and we may easily see that arguments used to promote the one relaxation lead at
once to the others. Why is there so much adultery, it will be said? And it will be answered,
because a man is tied for life to his wife. Yet I
think England is not yet prepared to see gentlemen
meeting two or three women, who have been successively their wives, in society; and such is the
case in Germany and the United States of America.
Nor are we prepared to see a fastidious gentleman
making the experiment, as to which of two or
three sisters he may prefer in succession as his
wife. Yet few can say that this will not be the

next demand of liberty. It is a liberty which exists in Germany, and in several of the United States.

There is in truth no species of moral relaxation so narrowly to be watched, as that which affects the intercourse between the sexes. And it has been thought a bad sign of the times when " Is habitus animorum fuit, ut pessimum facinus auderent pauci, plures vellent, omnes paterentur." And this applies far more to moral than political breaking of a law. You will find many men breaking the moral law, that should regulate their conduct towards women, who will neither cheat you, nor rob you—nay, they may even be (I have known such cases) kind husbands and fathers,— but they are not moral men, nor in any but the most vulgar sense *respectable*—a word, however, which appears now simply to mean rich.

But, fifthly, I say that there will be no hope of retracing our steps, or arresting this relaxation of morals when once begun,—" Vestigia nulla retrorsum." You break through the settled law as to incest. When are you to stop in picking and choosing your exceptions? Lord John Russell, who to my deep regret supported the proposed change, said with his usual straightforward frankness the law would be imperfect if it stopped at the wife's sister. It seems to me that brothers-in-law and brothers' widows, and uncles and nieces, as in Spain, must at least be allowed the same liberty !

Lastly, I ask, why is the happiness of every

home to be sacrificed to this caprice, for really it is no more, of a few, who are determined to marry some one person put out of their reach by law? Why are all men to lose their sisters-in-law because some disclaim that relationship? Why are all sisters-in-law now living with widowed brothers-in-law to be ordered either to quit or marry them? Above all, why is every man in the country who is free from the monomania of desiring a forbidden union to feel that his home is broken up by the snapping of the first link of moral restraint, to fear lest (as the next step) his own brother should desire his daughter in marriage, or look even to the reversion of his wife? Why is distrust to be sown where perfect love, frank familiarity, sweet and pure affection were before unrestrained? Why, lastly, is England to be selected for this blighting curse upon her homes? Ireland will have none of these relaxations; Scotland rejects them with abhorrence [7].

I have taken mere heathen ground in this letter. But by all the joys of that tie of real brotherhood which binds us to the sister of our wife; by all the aspirations of a high and holy morality, be the man's religious faith what it may; by all the horrors of an ever deepening, hopeless sinking

[7] The Bill last passed by the Commons would render it possible for an Irish or Scotch gentleman to have two wives at once; one, his wife's sister, at Holyhead or Carlisle, the other, an Irish or Scottish wife, for his English wife would in Ireland or Scotland be a concubine only.

into the abyss of cold cynical indifference as to the purity of our national life, I implore all men to aid us in resisting the proposed change of the home life of England.

A friend smiled when I said, "I would rather hear of the landing of 300,000 French at Dover than of the passing of this Bill." It was no exaggeration of my feelings. We can, and should, repel an external foe; but inward decay and rottenness will destroy us, sap our morals, and our only life worth having is at an end. Rome was burnt by the Gauls, but the Roman senate was unappalled. Hannibal caused her power to shrink to the dimensions of her walls, but a Roman nobly bought at full price the ground on which he had encamped. In the reign of Claudius, on the contrary, she seemed to command the known world, but that decree by which he was permitted to impugn her moral code showed that she was tottering to her fall. And most firmly do I believe, that the first breach in the social laws of England that govern marriage will be a clear indication of a moral failure, and a fall graver than any that ancient or modern history has recorded.

> Believe me,
> Dear Mr. Dean,
> Yours most faithfully,
> W. P. WOOD.

February, 1861.

LETTER II.

THE LAW VINDICATED ON SCRIPTURAL PRINCIPLES.

"But if any man seem to be contentious, we have no such custom, neither the churches of God."—1 COR. xi. 16.

DEAR MR. DEAN,

The first of these Letters was commenced during the late Session of Parliament, in the expectation that a Bill would be introduced for the purpose of altering the law as regards marriage within the prohibited degrees; but when, to my great satisfaction, I found the attempt was not to be made, I gladly postponed the preparation of my defence of our social institutions. In the mean time, the Rev. Dr. M'Caul has published a Letter addressed to myself, which commences as follows: "Your recently-published Speech on the Marriage Law, though obviously not intended as an answer to 'The Ancient Interpretation of Leviticus xviii. 18,' is yet considered by many, who share your views, as the best and most satisfactory answer to that pamphlet."

Certainly, Dr. M'Caul does me no more than

D

justice, when he says that my speech was not intended as any answer to his learned pamphlet referred to in the same passage. A great portion of
what I said was directed to establishing the proposition, which I hope I have by my first letter to
you, sir, established; viz. that though the Book of
Leviticus, or indeed all revealed law, had been
withheld from us, yet, if we had, as pagans, for
1200 years, defined the degrees of relationship
beyond which alone our society would recognize
marriage as lawful, it would be a fearful social
revolution to tamper with the definition that had
so regulated the social intercourse of every family
of the kingdom, and to begin to select cases in
which the law should be relaxed.

The only part of my address in which I came in
contact with the arguments of Dr. M‘Caul (in his
first pamphlet) was of course that which dealt with
the Scriptural sanction of our existing marriage
code. With that part of the subject, however, I
intend to deal more fully than time would allow in
a speech, in my present letter. I would rather
address you, sir, than Dr. M‘Caul, for two reasons :
firstly, I am not inclined naturally to controversy,
and I am less likely to fall into the snare that besets
all controversial writers, viz. a certain irritability
of temper towards the opponent, if I avoid engaging
in any direct conflict; and, secondly, I really find
(as I shall presently show) that nearly the whole of
Dr. M‘Caul's very learned labours are directed to a

point which, though important, is but a fragment of
the great religious question at issue, namely, to the
mere translation of a single verse of the marriage
code contained in the 18th chapter of Leviticus.
If that verse be translated one way, the unlawfulness of the marriages in question would not be
doubted; if it be translated in another way, then,
at the most, a doubt only is created; and my
argument throughout, in the speech referred to by
Dr. M'Caul, was, that if but a doubt existed, the
argument for abiding by the existing civil law,
sanctioned as it is by the Church of Christ having
at all times held the marriage in question to be
contrary to " God's law," must prevail. That point
of my argument I shall proceed to fortify in this
letter. I trust Dr. M'Caul will feel that I am offer-
ing no discourtesy to him in taking this course.
I had no previous intimation of his intention to
address a letter to me before its publication; and
I may fairly assume, therefore, that it is a form
adopted by him as convenient for a general reply
to the notice taken by others, much more than by
myself, of his first able pamphlet.

Let me, however, as a justification of my remark
with reference to the evil tendency of controversy,
quote, and leave to the consideration of Dr. M'Caul
in his calmer moments, the following passages of
his letter to me. After endeavouring to point out
some discrepancies of view in the various opponents
of a change of the law, as regards the interpretation

of the particular verse to which Dr. M'Caul mainly directs his attention, he says in page 2, "If the Marriage Law Defence Association be right, Dr. Pusey's interpretation must be rejected as erroneous. Zealous partisans may think that the end sanctifies the means, and that the circulation of a little perversion of the truth is no great matter, if it tend to the triumph of the good cause. But devout and thoughtful Christians will think differently, and feel that the diffusion of a false interpretation, however good the intentions, is a serious evil, and involves a responsibility which they would shrink from incurring."

I trust, sir, that neither you nor I may ever have any occasion to be ashamed of the support we have given to the Marriage Law Defence Association. That Association was formed to counteract the proceedings of some person or persons who have never yet ventured to give his or their name or names to the public, but who is or are indefatigable in exertion and purse in attempting to overthrow the existing law. Some proceedings of this anonymous opponent or opponents I have referred to in my first letter. I do not believe that Dr. M'Caul has seriously intended to accuse the large number of Clergy and of Christian noblemen and gentlemen who constitute the Marriage Law Defence Association of "thinking that the end sanctifies the means," or believing them to be less "devout and thoughtful Christians" than himself. It would be absurd to suppose that every individual of our numerous Association pledges himself on the one hand to an unconditional acceptance of every argument advanced in the publications which it authorizes, or on the other hand accepts Dr. Pusey's interpretation of Scripture contained in a publication not circulated by the Association, any more than that of Dr. M'Caul, as infallible.

Let me briefly re-state the arguments which I offered on the occasion referred to by Dr. M'Caul, with reference to the religious aspect of the question. My propositions are the following :—

I. The code of prohibited unions contained in the 18th chapter of Leviticus is binding on all men, and is not limited in its application to the Hebrew people.

II. The general guiding rule is laid down in verse 6 of that chapter, which prohibits approaching to any one that is " near of kin [1]."

III. " Nearness of kin " is there immediately explained by several examples, none of which go beyond the third degree, and such examples include relationship by affinity and by consanguinity without distinction. It will be shown also, that some one example, at least, is given of relationship within each of the three degrees, except (for obvious reasons)

---

[1] I am indebted to a very able MS paper of the Rev. Canon Woolcombe, of Exter, for the form in which I now state my third and fourth propositions.

that of great-grandparent to great-grand-child.

IV. That the examples are so given as to lead to a clear necessary inference, that the whole class, within the same degree of relationship as the particular example, is included in the prohibition.

V. That the Church of Christ from the earliest period so interpreted the Code, and held the marriage with the wife's sister to be forbidden by God's law; and in particular that our branch of the Church, in England (including always in that word the laity as well as clergy), has from the first so held.

VI. That the translation of a particular verse of the Code, viz. the 18th, even when translated after Dr. M'Caul's view, has not interfered with the above construction by the Church, or by any of the early writers, of the entire Code.

I. My first proposition, that the Code is binding on all nations, is readily proved by the following considerations. The Code is introduced by the preamble (verse 3) : " After the doings of the land of Egypt, wherein ye dwelt, shall ye not do : and after the doings of the land of Canaan, whither I bring you, shall ye not do : neither shall ye walk in their ordinances." Then follow the enactments of the Code, after which occur these words (vv. 24, 25) : " Defile not ye yourselves in any of these things: for in all these the nations are defiled which I cast out before you; and the land is defiled: therefore I do visit the iniquity thereof upon it, and the land itself vomiteth out her inhabitants." In the 28th verse similar language is used. Now the Canaanites could not be under any special law peculiar to the Israelites, for that is a contradiction in terms; yet the Canaanites were punished for the filthiness of these prohibited unions, and for the other abominations mentioned in the chapter. Therefore the prohibition must affect all men, and not merely the Israelites. The introductory third verse, which I have cited, shows clearly that the 24th and 25th verses cannot be restricted to the verses immediately preceding them, for the *whole Code* is introduced and followed by a denunciation of practices opposed to its provisions.

II. and III. My second and third propositions are patent on the perusal of the chapter—viz. that unions with those who are " near of kin " are prohibited (verse 6); and that examples are given of what is meant by " near of kin," which do not extend beyond the third degree; but which, at the same time, include cases of affinity and of consanguinity indifferently, and include some case of every possible relationship in such degree, with the single exception of great-grandparent and great-grandchild, as to whom, of course, no prohibition would be necessary after man's life had been shortened to its present ordinary duration. The simple and true conclusion I believe to be that of the early Fathers, and also of the early expositors in our Reformed Church, viz. that husband and wife become one flesh, and the nearness of kin therefore to one is nearness of kin to the other. It may be worth while to make this point a little clearer.

Let A. B. be the individual who is desirous of consulting the Code. The following Table represents his possible relations of the first, second, and third degrees, respectively.

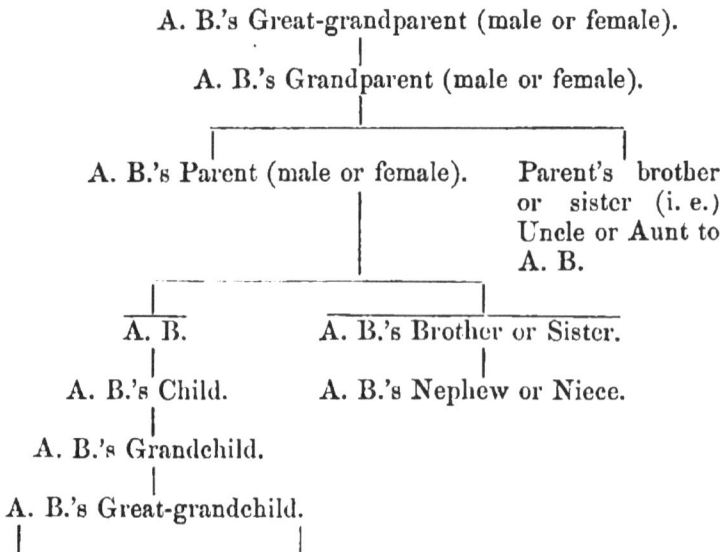

A. B.'s Great-grandparent (male or female).

A. B.'s Grandparent (male or female).

A. B.'s Parent (male or female).   Parent's brother or sister (i. e.) Uncle or Aunt to A. B.

A. B.   A. B.'s Brother or Sister.

A. B.'s Child.   A. B.'s Nephew or Niece.

A. B.'s Grandchild.

A. B.'s Great-grandchild.

The degrees are estimated by counting either upwards or downwards from A. B. in his direct line; and as to collaterals by counting up to the common ancestors and down again to A. B. Thus you count from the nephew to the brother, from the brother to the father, and from the father to A. B., making three degrees. Or again, from the uncle to the grandfather, from the grandfather to the father, from the father to A. B., making three degrees.

Let us then show how the degrees are dealt with by examples.

In the first degree we find mother and son dealt with by verse 7, then this is extended to the case of affinity, viz. a step-mother, by verse 8, then to the wife's mother by verse 17 (though that verse supposes the mother to have been first taken as wife). The case of a father and his son's wife is specified in verse 15. But there is no express mention of the case of father and daughter; for verse 17, though it would, perhaps, involve this case, is clearly directed to the case of a step-father and step-daughter.

As to the relationship in the second degree, or that of A. B.'s grandparents and his brother and sister respectively, the case of grandfather and granddaughter is dealt with in ver. 10. In verse 17 the prohibition is extended to the wife's granddaughter. There is no mention of the converse prohibition of marriage between grandson and grandmother, or between a husband and his wife's grandmother. The case of brother and sister, either of the whole or half blood, is provided for by verse 9, which seems indeed to include the case mentioned in verse 11; a point not unworthy of notice, as the prohibition is extended to the brother's wife by verse 16; and there is no direct

mention of the wife's sister, unless it be in verse
18, the interpretation of which has been so much
disputed.

As to relations in the third degree, viz. great-
grandparent, and uncle and aunt, and the common
cases of great-grandchild, nephew and niece, I
have observed that great-grandparent and great-
grandchild, probably from physical unlikelihood,
are not dealt with. The marriage of a nephew
with his paternal or maternal aunt is prohibited
in vv. 12 and 13, and is extended to an uncle's
wife by verse 14. There is no mention of the
converse case of the uncle and niece, whether by
consanguinity or affinity.

The result of the examination is this:—We find
in the first degree express prohibition of every
possible case between those related in that degree,
either by consanguinity or by affinity, except the
case of father and daughter, which is very in-
directly met by verse 17. We find in the second
degree, an express prohibition of union with a
granddaughter, either by consanguinity or by
affinity; but no express prohibition of the converse case of union with a grandmother.

We find express prohibition of union between
brother and sister of the whole or half blood, with
a repetition as to a father's wife's daughter be-
gotten by the father (in verse 11). We find an
express prohibition of marriage with a brother's
wife, but no express prohibition of union with a
wife's sister, unless verse 18 be interpreted as a

special and limited prohibition of that particular case. We have further to observe that the marriage with the wife's granddaughter, which is a relationship by affinity of the second degree, is prohibited in verse 17 on the very ground of her being "a near relation" of his wife, and such a union is said to be *wickedness*, whilst the union with the wife's sister (related in the same degree of nearness as a grandchild) is supposed by our opponents to be sanctioned by the verse next immediately following.

In the third degree we find no prohibition as to great-grandparents and great-grandchildren; but we find express prohibition of marriage between nephew and his paternal or maternal aunt, and between nephew and uncle's wife, whilst nothing is said as to uncle and niece, whether the relationship be by affinity or consanguinity, or even as to a man and his wife's aunt.

It appears to me that our opponents must either take the course of refusing to recognize any but *direct* prohibition, which would leave the cases perhaps of father and daughter, and certainly of the grandmother and of the niece, open amongst relations by consanguinity, and the cases of the wife's sister and of the aunt as regards relationship by affinity, whilst, nevertheless, by verse 17 union with the wife's grandmother and grandchild is prohibited; or they must admit the inference to the extent for which I contend, but then say that verse 18 affords a special exemption. In the first case the absurdity is involved of holding the general prohibition in verse 6, as to union between those who are " near of kin " (even confining it to consanguinity), to extend to a marriage of aunt and nephew, but not to that of uncle and niece, so that the relationship of the aunt to her nephew is to be held nearer than that of the uncle to his niece. If extended to affinity, then the wife's sister must be taken by them to be less near than the wife's grandchild or grandmother. In the other alternative, I again say, that which has been my argument from the first, you require a very clear permission to overthrow a series of strict enactments, all levelled against the iniquity of approaching to those who are " near of kin " to yourself or to your wife, and including prohibitions against union with relations, either by consanguinity or affinity, further removed than the wife's sister. If the permission be not clearly made out, either by a clear translation or a clear exposition of the 18th verse, then great is the hazard of those who would risk the denunciations contained in the 27th and 28th verses [2].

---

[2] I do not think it necessary to dwell on the *direction* (contained in another portion of Scripture) to marry a deceased brother's wife, where the brother has left no child. Dr. M'Caul does not contend, nor would any sound expositor contend, that a distinct prohibition is revoked by an exception, beyond the extent of the excepted case. Now the prohibition as to the brother's wife is happily clear from all cavil, and the injunction in the excepted case is enforced by penalties, as if it were foreseen that it would be reluctantly and with repugnance observed.

It will be observed I speak of two classes of doubts—first, as to translation; secondly, as to exposition and effect. Dr. M'Caul conceives that he has triumphantly proved his case, when he has accumulated authorities to prove the *translation* given in the text of our authorized version to be preferable to that given in the margin. He cites passages from the early Fathers, especially dwelling on Jerome and Augustine, to prove that they interpreted the verse as he does, viz. as prohibiting marriage with a wife's sister during the life of the wife; and thence conceives that such a translation can only be expounded as giving direct permission to marry the wife's sister after the decease of the wife.

Now I shall certainly not follow Dr. M'Caul's example, by attributing that bad faith to him which he so unpleasantly and uncharitably imputes to his opponents, when he imagines he has shown them to be illogical in their reasoning, or inaccurate in their history [3]; but I do say that a most complete mystification of the argument of his opponents, and misrepresentation of its effect, has been the result of Dr. M'Caul's mixing together the questions of translation and exposition. For those ancient writers, and many of the modern

[3] See besides the passage before cited as to "zealous partisans circulating a little perversion of Scripture that the good cause may triumph," his statement as to Mr. Baddely insinuating without directly stating what is contrary to fact, page 9 of his letter to myself.

authors who agree with Dr. M'Caul in his translation, nevertheless concur with us in holding the
marriage in question to be forbidden by the Levitical Code, as will appear more fully hereafter.

Dr. M'Caul, in page 5, rather ingeniously lays
hold of the interpretation of the 18th verse as a
prohibition of polygamy, and says that all who so
interpret it, " and *infer* that on the death of the
first wife a second marriage is lawful, help to esta-
blish his third point, the inference from the words
in her *lifetime,* as an obvious and legitimate conclusion." The fallacy here is so obvious, that I
am surprised it did not occur to Dr. M'Caul that
there are no such persons as he mentions. Those
who read the 18th verse as a prohibition of polygamy, do not *infer* any thing as to the lawfulness
of a second marriage after the first wife's death.
No such inference is necessary, because a second
marriage is nowhere forbidden. But *the question*
with Dr. M'Caul is, whether when we have proved
a prohibition in the preceding verses of the chapter
by the course of reasoning I have used, there can
be found a licence to marry within the prohibited
degrees in a verse that merely (even in his translation) prohibits a special kind of polygamy. It
will be seen as I proceed that this translation may
be granted to Dr. M'Caul, and has been assumed
by numerous authorities, who reject utterly the
inference he would draw from it.

That I may not misrepresent this singular blun-

der, I will quote from the Doctor's letter to myself
the following passage (page 49):—" Moreover this
translation, *which is in truth an interpretation*, has
become the public teaching of the whole Church of
England and Ireland in all parts of the world. It
is the translation read in churches, and by the
translators intended to be read, and not the mar-
ginal version. It has remained undisturbed in its
place of honour for two centuries and a half, acquiesced in by sovereign, clergy, and people, and
therefore appears to me to express more certainly
the mind of the whole English Church than the
99th Canon, which was never confirmed by Parliament. And this is one reason why I cannot receive your statement that the Church of England
always held, and still holds, that marriage with a
deceased wife's sister is unlawful. No doubt the
Anglo-Saxon Church received the law as laid down
by Gregory the Great. When the English Church
lay prostrate at the feet of Rome it received Roman
Canon Law and all her prohibited degrees. But
the Eighth Henry's Acts of Parliament no more
represent the decision of the Church of England
than the counter Act of Philip and Mary or the
modern Act of 1835. Archbishop Parker's Table
of Prohibited Degrees was the act of one individual,
no more involving the judgment of the English
Church than Whitgift's sanction of the Lambeth
Articles. The only authentic declaration of the
English Reformed Clergy is the 99th Canon of the

Convocation of the Province of Canterbury, 1603-4,
subsequently adopted by the Convocation of York,
but which never received the confirmation of the
laity in Parliament, not even in the Act of 1835.
Indeed, so far is that Act from confirming that
Canon, that it contradicts its main proposition by
legitimating already contracted marriages which
this Canon pronounces 'incestuous and not lawful
... and void from the beginning.' *Against this
Canon of such partial authority is to be weighed
the later declaration of the Church of England
contained in the authorized version of* 1611, *accepted by the whole Church, the sovereign, the
clergy, and the laity, and appointed to be read in
the public service.*"

I think the above passage plainly shows that
Dr. M'Caul conceives the *translation* of the authorized version to be conclusive in its *exposition*
(or as he terms it interpretation), and that he even
assigns such efficiency to this translation, as to
regard it (in the last sentence above quoted) in the
light of a repeal of the Canon of 1603-4, for one
does not otherwise see the force of his observation
that this " declaration of the Church of England "
has been accepted by the Clergy. The translation
of the Bible is, in other words, supposed in 1611
to have got rid, by a side-wind, of a solemn Canon
passed about eight years previously, and the King
and Parliament are taken to have acquiesced in
this ingenious contrivance.

The above passage will be again referred to, in respect of its most singular mistakes both as to our Ecclesiastical and our Civil Law. I shall then show that our Civil Courts, in the time of Charles II., held marriage with the wife's sister to be void, on the very ground that it was within the Levitical degrees. But what I am at this moment concerned with is the quiet assumption made by Dr. M'Caul, that the translation which he advocates, and in which he is doubtless supported by the authorized version, and by many authorities ancient and modern, at once settles the question of the lawfulness of marriage with a deceased wife's sister. Now so far is this from being the case, that Dr. M'Caul has not been able to produce a single Christian writer, prior to the Reformation, who has intimated an expression even of doubt as to the illegality of the marriage in question. He was distinctly challenged to do this in a learned pamphlet, published by Dr. Pusey in 1860, called "God's Prohibition of the Marriage with a Deceased Wife's Sister not to be set aside by an Inference from a Restriction of Polygamy among the Jews." Dr. M'Caul must have read this pamphlet, for in page 17 of his letter to me he quotes with approbation a passage from page 37 of the pamphlet. And almost immediately preceding the passage quoted by Dr. M'Caul, viz. in page 36, Dr. Pusey says, " But no Christian writer, I believe, can be found for fifteen centuries (except that

E

Diodorus mentioned by St. Basil) who had any doubt that the marriage with the deceased wife's sister was forbidden by the law of God." This challenge Dr. M'Caul has not accepted, nor has he made the attempt, which I believe would have been a vain one, to find the least support from Christian antiquity in favour of his *inference* from verse 18, as distinguished from its translation. Yet this surely was the very gist of the case. Because if the received translation be proved to be correct, and yet the inference derived from it, so far from being clear (as it ought to be) in favour of a licence to marry a deceased wife's sister, was never recognized, nor the verse regarded as affording such licence by the Church either before, or (as I shall presently show, by the Church of England at least) after the Reformation, then the whole of Dr. M'Caul's learned argument for the translation may be admitted by the opponents of a change in the law of our Church, including in that term (as I always do) the laity, without any fear of their interpretation of Scripture being shaken. On the contrary, Dr. M'Caul, in fact, only makes his own case the worse, when he proves (as he thinks) an all but universal acceptation from the earliest times of *his* translation, if there co-existed amongst Christians an equally universal belief that the marriage in question was nevertheless prohibited by God's law, and if our own Ecclesiastical and Lay tribunals, with his translation before them, still held the

marriage objected to to be within the Levitical
degrees. There is certainly a very feeble, though
I doubt not an honest attempt of Dr. M'Caul to
fasten on Augustine his own notion that his translation, by inference, settles the whole question.
In his letter to me, page 3, he says, " With regard
to Augustine it is plain from his words that he did
receive the inference. What he considers forbidden is, ' Sororem sorori superducere.'" He
then cites a passage from a different work of
Augustine where he says, " Et nostris quidem
temporibus, ac more Romano nec superducere
licet, ut amplius habeat quam unam viventem;"
and he adds this singular reasoning : " As Augustine therefore believed that to *superduce* a
second wife, was to take a second wife whilst the
first was still alive, and that it was lawful (whatever he thought of the expediency) to have a
second wife when the first was dead, so when he
uses the same word respecting two sisters 'Sororem
sorori noluit superducere,' he means that it is
unlawful to have a second wife whilst the first is
living, *but that when the first is dead it is lawful.*"
The words in italics beg the whole question. The
argument is that the 18th verse, however translated, does not abrogate the law against marrying
those who are " near of kin" as contained in the
6th verse; and that an inferential permission is
not given to marry the wife's sister after the wife's
death, by a prohibition to marry her during the

wife's lifetime. But Dr. M'Caul says that Augustine must have held such an inference, because he adopted the translation. Now it is well known that Basil (in 375, if Dr. M'Caul wishes that to be the date) adopted the translation (as Dr. M'Caul triumphantly remarks), but wholly rejected the inference, as our Church has since done. And what possible ground can the fact of Augustine adopting the translation afford for arguing that he necessarily adopted Dr. M'Caul's inference? Surely his using the same word " superducere" to express the same thing, when speaking of polygamy generally, as when speaking of a prohibition of a particular form of it, does not prove that he inferred from that prohibition a licence to marry a wife's sister after the wife's death. The lawfulness of a second marriage, *simpliciter*, being abundantly recognized in Scripture, the prohibition of polygamy simply left that right untouched. If Dr. M'Caul could show that the Christian Church ever recognized as lawful a single marriage with a deceased wife's sister, he would do something, but without this his whole argument as to the translation of the words rather leads to a contrary result; for the Church, though adopting (in that case) his translation, yet rejects his inference as to its effect.

Having said so much on the confusion of the argument as to translation, with the argument as to exposition, and intending, as I do, to show that the inferential permission to marry a wife's sister, after the wife's death, has been uniformly rejected by our Church, I need hardly add one word more as to the translation itself. I will simply say that a sect of the Jews, the Karaites, read the 18th verse as meaning " thou shalt not add one wife to another,"—" a wife to her sister" being a common Hebraism for adding one thing to another, even as applied to inanimate things, and so translated in every other passage (about thirty times) where it occurs, and so rendered in our margin[4]. Many learned men have taken the same view. I am bound to do justice to Dr. M'Caul's research, and to say that he has produced a powerful body of evidence in favour of a contrary translation, and if the matter rested here, and was concluded by translation merely, then though a reverent man might hesitate in a matter of such deep importance, yet less scrupulous minds might be satisfied. There remains, however, even then a question to whom the words " in *her* lifetime " refer. If they refer to the wife's sister, then it is an absolute

---

[4] The objection that Polygamy could not have been prohibited because holy men of old had more than one wife at a time, is not to my mind conclusive. Abraham, Isaac, and Joseph had each but one wife at a time. The case of Abraham's concubine Hagar was peculiar, and certainly not favourably viewed either in the Old Testament, or by St. Paul in the New. Jacob was tricked into his first marriage. Elkanah's case was certainly one not attended with blessing. David and Solomon openly transgressed the distinct law against the King's multiplying wives. The subject, however, is too long for such a publication as the present.

prohibition to marry the wife's sister during all her (the sister's) lifetime, and I think Cranmer's Bible, cited in Dr. M'Caul's letter to Mr. Lyall, adopts that view; but the translation is, after all, a fragment only of the case, and therefore I hasten to the second question, namely, Is the inference from the 18th verse, however translated, clear as a permission to marry the wife's sister after the wife's death?

Dr. M'Caul says that the Jews believed they might contract such marriages, whilst the heathen Romans were also allowed like liberty, therefore the Christian opponents of such marriage are bound to show any teaching of the Primitive Church to the contrary of so established a custom. Addressing me (in page 6) he says, if in lack of New Testament evidence I could have begun with the immediate followers of the Apostles, and continued the chain of evidence, he would have accepted the antiquity and catholicity of the evidence as demonstrative of an Apostolical repeal of Leviticus xviii. 18. It will be observed that he assumes the verse to be a conclusive permission. I am not quite sure that I should go so far as Dr. M'Caul in my respect, great though it be, for such evidence. I certainly have never contended that less than absolute Scriptural authority would repeal, or rather explain, a clear text of Scripture. In my view of the subject there is nothing to repeal but the 6th verse, which, if it were to be repealed, would have been so by

Scripture itself. But I ask how, if Jews and
.Heathens recognized such marriages as lawful, the
quiet acquiescence of the Christian world in the
conclusion that the 18th verse does not authorize
such marriages can be explained? I had said
that Basil, about 350, remonstrated against such a
perversion of the verse, and that we did not hear
of any earlier remonstrance before, because such a
marriage was not heard of amongst Christians.
I thought myself justified in saying this from
Basil's assertion that such marriages were against
custom. Dr. M'Caul attempts to confine that expression to some local custom. Why, he himself
reminds me of the Council of Eliberis in 305, and
tells me that St. Basil's letter was written in 375.
You have, therefore, a law of the Church seventy
years before, directed probably against Heathen
practices, passed, in a place far from Basil as west is
from east, on the same subject. When Basil refers
to custom it is of course of general Christian custom,
as distinguished from Heathen customs—just as
St. Paul uses this identical word, when he says,
" If any man seem to be contentious, we have no
such custom, neither the churches of God [5]." I use
Basil as a *witness* of a pre-established custom. But
Dr. M'Caul reminds me further (and I thank him) of
the 19th Apostolic Canon, about A.D. 300, and the
decree of the Council of Neo-Cæsarea in 314, on the
subject of marriage with a wife's brother. The

[5] 1 Cor. xi. 16.

decree of the Emperor Constantius in 355 is also
remarkable evidence of the feeling of the early
Christians, for as soon as Christianity is established
we find the Heathen practice is at once repealed.
Now I freely admit to Dr. M'Caul that if I were
advocating a repeal of God's law by the traditions
of men, I should be open to his argument "ad in-
vidiam," when he refers to superstitious notions
entertained at the same period, and asks me if I am
prepared to accept such superstitions. This is,
however, but an old fallacy. The interpretation of
Scripture (as distinguished from mere translation)
being the question, reference to ancient and continuous acceptance of a passage, or to ancient and
continuous practice, which indicate the sense attri-
buted to the passage, is most valuable. This Dr.
M'Caul allows, and indeed relies upon with regard
to his translation of the 18th verse. The circumstance that the same writings, or the practice of
the same age, afford evidence of superstitious
usages also, does not diminish the weight of their
evidence as to the *fact*, whether Christians did or
did not hold the marriage with a deceased wife's
sister to be contrary to God's law. The fact that
the large majority of Christians from the time of
the Apostles down to the present time have
deduced the doctrine of the Trinity from Scripture
will remain an important fact, whether or not the
same Christians have from an early time held
various superstitious notions irreconcilable with

Scripture. Our Church does not accept any of the Fathers as authorities overruling Scripture, but claims them as witnesses to what has been the general assent of the Church from the time of the Apostles with regard to the interpretation of Scripture.

The case, then, stands thus. We have, as early as the commencement of the third century, direct testimony that the customary practice of Christians was against the marriage in question, though their heathen relatives allowed them. We have the custom of Christendom, I say, referred to by Basil on this head; and shortly before his testimony, and almost as soon as Christianity had been firmly established, we have a law of the Emperor Constantius, which never would have been enacted had not this Christian custom been well established also. To say that Constantius was an Arian, is an observation the force of which I confess myself unable to appreciate. The question of incestuous unions is a Scriptural and social question lying far deeper than any differences of doctrine, however important in themselves. It is, happily, not in this country a Low Church or High Church question. Such unions are abhorred in Scotland by every denomination of Christians, and in our own country by men of every division of opinion in Church matters.

There is no Christian writer before the Reformation who has been produced by Dr. M'Caul as supporting these marriages, notwithstanding many writers favour his translation of the 18th verse of Leviticus.

But how has the Church of England on this subject interpreted Scripture? Dr. M'Caul (in the passage I have already cited) says, "No doubt the Anglo-Saxon Church received the law as laid down by Gregory the First. When the English Church lay prostrate at the feet of Rome it received Rome's Canon Law, and all her prohibited degrees." He will not, therefore, require me to prove that down to the Reformation, at least, our Church regarded the marriages in question as prohibited. In the word "Church" I include, of course, the laity. No doubt corruptions had crept in, by which the prohibitions had been extended beyond the Levitical degrees. It is to be feared this was done with a view of augmenting the revenues of the Pope by dispensations, but until the licence granted by the infamous Alexander VI. to the King of Portugal to marry a wife's sister, dispensations had never been granted to authorize marriage within the Levitical degrees. In Henry the Eighth's case all the foreign Universities were unanimous in opinion as to the unlawfulness *by God's Law* of marriage with a deceased brother's widow, and many of them distinguished between marriages forbidden by the law of God, and those forbidden by the rule of the Church. The real point of difficulty in that case was, whether or not the rule applied where there had been no consummation of the first marriage. Whilst on the subject of dispensation I may notice that, as late as in 1723, the Parliament of Paris, on an " Appel comme d'abus," in the Marquis of Sailly's case, declared his child by a deceased wife's sister illegitimate, notwithstanding the marriage had been had under a dispensation from the Pope, on the ground that the Pope could not dispense with God's law.

But how has our Church dealt with the subject since the Reformation?

Dr. M'Caul, in his letter to Mr. Lyall, page 21, deals with this part of the case in a very singular manner. After quoting several Protestant versions of the 18th verse, which render it as a prohibition against marrying a wife's sister during the lifetime of *the former*, he says, " In Cranmer's Bible the translation is similar, ' Thou shalt not take a woman and her sister else to vex her, that thou woldest uncover her secretes as long as she liveth.' " I confess this seems to me a very different translation, for it appears to refer " as long as she liveth " to the sister, and not to the wife. But this is not all. Dr. M'Caul adds, " And to this translation Cranmer adhered, as may be seen in the ' Reformatio Legum Ecclesiasticarum,' which expresses the joint judgment of Cranmer, Goodwin, Cox, May, Peter Martyr, and Rowland Taylor. Chap. v. is, ' Enumeratio personarum in Levitico prohibitarum,—In Levitico dispositæ

personæ citantur his nominibus, mater, noverca,
. . . filia, filia uxoris, soror uxoris.' In the revision
of Cranmer's Bible by Cuthbert, Bishop of Durham,
and Ridley in 1541, the same translation is retained, and a reference given in the margin to
Gen. xxix., showing that they understood it of
simultaneous marriage with two sisters." Why,
if any thing can be clear, it is that in the passage
cited by Dr. M'Caul, Cranmer (fortified, as the
Doctor says, by the other Reformers whom he
refers to) places the wife's sister in exactly the
same position as the mother, step-mother, &c., as
I shall presently show, our Law, both Ecclesiastical and Civil, has never failed to do. It
seems to me, however, that the fallacy running
through the whole argument of Dr. M'Caul, and
those who follow him, is this : that a special prohibition is a licence to do any thing not included
within the special words of restriction. On this
principle the Eighth Commandment, " Thou shalt
not commit adultery," would be a licence to commit fornication.

But the conclusive point on the view entertained
by both clergy and laity, since the Reformation, is
to be found in the fact that, though the 32 Hen.
VIII. c. 38, authorizes interference by the Lay
Courts of the realm with the Ecclesiastical Court,
when that Court deals with questions of marriages
beyond its jurisdiction, it expressly excepts the
case of marriages either otherwise contrary to

God's Law or within the Levitical degrees [6]; and this being the only exception, nevertheless the Courts of Common Law uniformly down to the last conclusive decree of Fenton *v.* Livingstone (the judgments in which, so far as they bear on this point, are given in the Appendix), have held that marriage with a deceased wife's sister is within the Levitical degrees, and therefore void.

The clergy, of course, are further bound by the Canon of 1611; but both clergy and laity are bound by the statutes as interpreted by the highest courts of the realm, and, therefore, my proposition is established, that the Church of England has for all time held these marriages to be prohibited by the Levitical degrees. Hence will be seen what a singular mistake Dr. M'Caul makes in supposing in the passage I have cited, from page 50 of his letter to me, that the *translation* of the 18th verse in our Bible has released either clergy or laity from the effect of the Statute as well as Canon Law, which both expressly hold such marriages invalid, as being within the prohibition contained in the 18th chapter of Leviticus.

But Dr. M'Caul, in the same passage, falls into the singularly prevailing error of supposing that the Act of 1835 rendered valid marriages already contracted, and which the Canon Law declared to be incestuous. I have already shown, in my previous letter, that the Act of 1835 did no such thing.

[6] See the Statute cited in my first letter.

It prevented the calling in question the legitimacy of the offspring of marriages then existing, and applied to all such marriages, though the parents might be living, the same rule that our Courts of Common Law had always applied when one parent had died; but it left the marriage invalid, and the parents punishable for incest. I again appeal to the judgment in Fenton v. Livingstone as showing that at no time has any such marriage been otherwise than invalid and incestuous in England.

Let me here repeat, for it cannot be too often stated, seeing the persevering efforts made by the Anonymous Society for altering our marriage law to mislead the public, that the Law of England has never made any difference between the degrees of incest,—that we are now invited for the first time to pick and choose from the prohibited degrees. If a man before Lord Lyndhurst's Act married his own mother or sister, and had a child by her, yet after the death of either parent nothing (short of an Act of Parliament) could declare the child illegitimate. After Lord Lyndhurst's Act, the children of any such odious union then existing would have been also freed for ever from the possibility of being declared illegitimate, though both their parents were alive. That Act, however, provided, in my judgment most wisely and humanely, that, in future, the legitimate status should not be acquired by the form of marriage being gone through in any case of incestuous marriages. From the beginning to the end of that Act no difference is made between the marriage with a mother, a sister, or a sister-in-law; and if it were repealed to-morrow, all those marriages would be *equally* void; but the children could not, after the death of either parent, be *declared* illegitimate.

This letter has become longer than I intended, from my desire to leave nothing of importance untouched. I do not enter into the Hebrew disquisitions of Dr. M'Caul. To a printed copy of my speech I added an appendix, containing observations by a writer of great ability, to show what might be said on the other side on that head. I do not profess any critical knowledge of Hebrew. The learned author of the tract I quoted is quite competent to defend himself, if he think it necessary, even though his "manifest ignorance" is assumed by Dr. M'Caul as proved by some printer's blunders in setting up Hebrew type, a style of controversy to be greatly deprecated. But I must be allowed to repeat an observation I made in my speech at Willis's Rooms : " That it is singular we should be called upon as Christians to follow the Jewish Rabbis in our interpretation of Scripture." I commented on the Jewish system of narrowing God's law by their traditions. To my great astonishment, Dr. M'Caul (page 36 of his letter to me) disputes this proposition, and says, "that so far from narrowing God's law, the great and fundamental sin of the Jewish traditions is the *adding* to the law, and making it a burden grievous to be borne by *forbidding what God has not forbidden.*" (The italics are Dr. M'Caul's.) Now certainly, as a mere English reader of my Bible, I had understood the Sermon on the Mount, as well as the denunciation of the traditions illustrated by the " Corban," to be reprimands by our Blessed Lord of the narrow view that the Jews took of the Divine law. " Ye have heard that it hath been said, Thou shalt love thy neighbour, and hate thine enemy [7]," I always understood to refer to their traditional interpretation of the command to love our neighbour ; as our opponents hold of verse 18, in the 18th of Leviticus, that the prohibition of one case allows all others. The Rabbinical interpreters said, " We are told to love our neighbours, therefore we may hate our enemies." Thus it is now said, " We are told not to marry the wife's sister in her lifetime," therefore we may marry her afterwards [8]. But as I am no Hebrew scholar I will call in the aid of Lightfoot to show how the Rabbis narrowed the law on the matter of divorce, a subject nearly akin to that in hand. That they also added superstitious rules, and so endeavoured by rigour in outward observances to compensate for laxity of moral conduct, is no doubt very true, but is no answer to my argument.

[7] Matt. v. 43.

[8] See Dr. Pusey's very learned pamphlet of 1860 above referred to. He observes that a heresy was built on the words, " Sit Thou on my right hand *until* I make Thine enemies Thy footstool," as if our Lord's kingdom was then to end.

Lightfoot, in a comment on the Sermon on the Mount [9], contained in his Hebrew and Talmudical Examples, says, " The School of Hillel said, ' If the wife cook her husband's food illy by over-salting or over-roasting it, she is to be put away.' " And a little lower down he says, " But not to relate all the things for which they pronounce a wife to be divorced (among which they produce some things that modesty allows not to be repeated), let it be enough to mention that of Rabbi Ahikah instead of all. R. Ahikah saith, If any man sees a woman handsomer than his own wife, he may put her away, because it is said, ' If she find not favour in his eyes.' "

And for this passage Lightfoot cites the Mishna. I think I have shown that the Rabbis are not safe interpreters of their own law for Christians.

I have purposely also passed by Dr. M'Caul's list of foreign divines since the Reformation. I deal with an English question. I do not consider Luther, who assumed a power to license polygamy, a very safe guide upon such a point. It is more interesting to know how the Kirk of Scotland has dealt with the subject. In 1643 the Assembly of Divines at Westminster resolved, " A man may not marry any of the wife's kindred nearer in blood than he may of his own, nor a woman of her husband's kindred nearer in blood than she may of her own." This is still the doctrine of the Kirk,

[9] Matt. v. 31.

notwithstanding their translation of the 18th verse agrees with that of our version and of Dr. M'Caul[1].

With regard to the Clergy of Scotland, I believe them to be all but unanimous on the subject. With regard to our English Clergy, I think that the small minority who favour a change in the law, would do well to consider the position in which all Clergymen will be placed if the law be changed, whilst the prohibiting Canon remains; and whether disunion between the Church and State on so grave a subject must not eventually and speedily lead to the entire separation of the two. This has been so much felt by Parliament, that in one Bill it was proposed to insert a clause freeing the Clergyman from the necessity of celebrating such a union. Certainly it would be a singular anomaly to compel a Clergyman to incur the Ecclesiastical penalties consequent on a breach of the Canon.

I have now accomplished what is to me in all respects a very irksome task. It is irksome to me at all times to commit my thoughts to writing. Controversy, again, affords no pleasure to me. Few of us can escape the evils that environ the disputant. Few, alas! can bear in mind, in the heat of controversy, Hooker's truly Christian warning, "That an hour will come when a few

[1] The New School Presbyterians of the United States about a year ago passed in their general assembly a Resolution against marriage with a deceased wife's sister, and deposed a minister who had so married.

words spoken in charity will outweigh whole volumes written with disdainful sharpness of wit." I can only ask pardon of all whom I may offend, whilst endeavouring to uphold what I firmly believe to be God's law. I desire not by sharpness of tone to offend against His highest law, even the great law of love.

If we had no revelation of His will, I believe that we should commit an act fatal to the peace of society in abrogating a law that has regulated our homes since we became one people; but if there be any weight whatever in the constant acknowledgment from our first becoming Christians, not merely by our Church, but by our Parliament and our judges, that the unions in question are contrary to " God's law," surely every Christian legislator will pause before he advises the nation to incur a risk of judgments so fearful as those that overwhelmed the offending heathens of old; even if in doubt he will ponder, well and seriously and with prayer, the question, whether the supposed evil to be remedied be such as to demand a remedy so perilous.

Believe me,

Dear Mr. Dean,

Yours most faithfully,

W. P. WOOD.

February, 1861.

POSTSCRIPT.

SINCE the above letter was written, a pamphlet has been put into my hands which purports to be written by Viscount Gage. I protest against the tone of it, by which he endeavours to throw, what he conceives, the odium of the opposition to the change of our law, on the clergy. For though I conceive it to be a glory, and not a shame, that our national Church has adhered to the sound interpretation of Leviticus on this subject, yet as a matter of fact Lord Gage may see, even by the names of the members of our Society, that the laity are quite as anxious for the preservation of the law as the clergy. He speaks of the " ingenious opponent prelates," and ends his somewhat violent invective on the Church of England by asking, " Will the House of Lords continue to show more deference to antiquated Church laws than to the report of their own Commissioners and the repeated votes of the representatives of the people ? " I will venture to ask, will the House of Lords venture to outrage the moral

feeling of Scotland and Ireland, which the representatives of the people have respected ? If not,
whether Lord Gage will support a bill which will
enable a man to have two wives, one in Scotland
or Ireland, and one in England? His lordship
says, " Every example given in Leviticus, with the
one exception of the maternal aunt, is either of
blood relations, or of one imported and installed
as a member of the family." I do not quite
understand this passage, for a maternal aunt *is* a
blood relation, and must not therefore be excepted.
But possibly the uncle's wife is meant (verse 14).
I do not myself see how it is made out that any of
the three cases in verse 17 are necessarily imported
or installed as members of the family, and certainly
they are not blood relations. I can, however,
vouch for the sister-in-law being very frequently
" installed as a member of the family," and
thousands of them would be driven from their
homes by any alteration of the law. Lord Gage
thinks a sister-in-law is " by fiction of law called
sister; and is in fact, and on a matter of incest, as
entirely unrelated to him as she was before."
That is simply begging the question, a remark
which I may apply to a great portion of his lordship's letter. As far as there are arguments to
meet, I think I have dealt with them. His lordship will probably in the House of Lords meet
both with " opponent prelates " and opponent
laymen who will do them more ample justice.

Pages 15 and 16 afford strong instances of the
inexpediency of such discussions as the present.
I will not follow his lordship upon such a ground,
nor answer his jests upon our Marriage Service.

APPENDIX TO LETTER I.

FENTON *v.* LIVINGSTONE.   LIVINGSTONE *v.* LIVINGSTONE.

*Extracts from the Speeches of the Law Lords in delivering
Judgment.*

LORD BROUGHAM.

" WAS the marriage, then, of the respondent's parents
such that the law of Scotland could recognize its validity
in dealing with the rights of the issue of it to take real
estates by inheritance? First of all, let us consider if it
was legal in the country where contracted, and where the
parties had their domicile. It was clearly illegal by the
law of England. That law treated it as incestuous by the
rules of the Ecclesiastical Court, which alone has cognizance of this objection to a marriage. It could not be
questioned, except during the lives of both husband and
wife; but it was illegal, and if questioned while both
parties were alive, it must have been declared void *ab
initio.* And why? Because it was contrary to law. The
circumstance of one party to it having died before this dispute arose, and before it was questioned, did not make the
marriage legal, though it precluded the possibility of setting it aside; and the son was issue, not of a lawful marriage, but of a marriage which could not be questioned

with effect, according to the rules of the Ecclesiastical
Court, that Court alone having jurisdiction upon the question, by the rules which govern the Temporal Courts. But
they hold the same principles on this subject as the Ecclesiastical, and would act upon them if they could entertain
the question. Indeed, the 5 & 6 Will. IV., c. 54 (Lord
Lyndhurst's Act), proceeds upon the ground that marriages within the forbidden degrees of affinity are void if
questioned, void because illegal; and enacts that hence-
forth they shall be *ipso facto* void, and not voidable by any
proceeding. And why? Because they are within the
forbidden degrees, that is, because prohibited by law. It
is unnecessary to inquire whether a marriage so void, if
questioned in England before the Act, but prevented from
being questioned by the course of procedure in the English
court, could be questioned in Scotland, if the Scotch and
English law differed upon the grounds of the objection,
because the Scotch law is so much more stringent on the
subject than the English, holding all marriages within the
forbidden degrees not only to be incestuous, but severely
punishable, even capitally."

"If the lex loci contractus were to prevail absolutely,
and a marriage good in a country where it took place, and
where the party claiming it was born, were to make that
party inheritable in Scotland, then, uncle and niece marrying in a foreign country with papal dispensation, their
issue might claim to take a Scotch estate and Scotch
honours, although, had the marriage been contracted in
Scotland, the parties might have been capitally convicted,
and sentenced to death or transportation, as in the case of
Stewart and Wallace."

LORD CRANWORTH.

"Their decision proceeded on the ground that, as the marriage took place in England between parties domiciled there, the law of England must decide whether the marriage was or was not valid, and whether the issue of that marriage was or was not capable of entering as heir of the body of his parents lawfully procreate. They came to the conclusion that by the law of England the marriage was valid, and that the respondent was the eldest son of that marriage lawfully procreate, and therefore was entitled to succeed to the lands in question. After giving to this subject my best attention, I have come, though not without some fluctuation of opinion, to the conclusion that the Court of Session was wrong in treating this marriage as a valid marriage by the law of England, and in treating the respondent as the legitimate son of Thurstanus for the purpose of the Scotch succession. The stat., 25 Hen. VIII., c. 22, s. 4, expressly enacts, inter alia, that no man shall marry his deceased wife's sister, and, in case of any marriage being contracted in violation of that prohibition, the Ecclesiastical Court, with whom, in this country, jurisdiction on this subject exclusively rests, would declare any such marriage to be void. It is true that, by the construction put on that statute, no inquiry as to the validity of marriage could be instituted by the Ecclesiastical Court after the marriage itself had come to an end by the death of one of the parties; so that, inasmuch as the Temporal Courts had no jurisdiction, the issue would succeed to the estate of a deceased parent, as his or her heir, if no proceedings had been taken in the lifetime of both parents to declare the marriage void. I say to declare it void,—for it must be observed that the Court had no authority to interfere actively to dissolve any marriage validly contracted, but only to declare what the law was as to the alleged marriage,—the marriage de facto, as it was called,—to declare that there never was any marriage ; to declare it 'fuisse et esse invalidum ab initio.' That such a result must have followed a proceeding in the Ecclesiastical Court, calling in question the second marriage of Thurstanus, is a matter which can admit of no doubt. But if so, how can the true character of the marriage be altered by the accident of whether any third person did or did not think it worth while to call it in question? It is not the proceeding in the Ecclesiastical Court which made such a marriage void; the Court in this country could not affect by its decree a valid marriage; its jurisdiction was only of a declaratory nature, that is, to declare the legal invalidity of an act already complete, but which was not what it purported to be—a marriage.

" Where it has been the policy of the law of any country to prohibit marriage under any circumstances, the prohibition attaches to the subjects of that country wherever they go. It was on this principle that the case of the *Sussex Peerage* was decided. The marriage there was clearly valid according to the laws of the country where it was contracted; but it was held in this House that the Royal Marriage Act having prescribed certain steps by which alone the descendants of King George II. could contract marriage, the laws of this country would prevail wherever the marriage was contracted."

LORD WENSLEYDALE.

" My opinion is, that by the law of England the marriage of a widower with his deceased wife's sister was always as illegal and invalid as a marriage with a sister, daughter, or mother was. This appears to be clear by the decision in the well-considered case of Reg. *v.* Chadwick, and Reg. *v.* St. Giles, in which the several statutes and authorities prior to Lord Lyndhurst's Act, 5 & 6 Will. IV., c. 54, are commented upon and considered. It was always deemed as being within the prohibited and Levitical degrees; but, from the peculiarity that the question of the validity of marriage (with reference to this objection of being within the Levitical degrees) was matter of Ecclesiastical cognizance, and cognizable in the Spiritual Court alone, it could not be questioned after the death of either party, for it could not be dissolved by the Court then, as death had already dissolved it; nor could the issue be bastardized, though the survivor might be visited with the ecclesiastical censures. But the marriage was still an unlawful and forbidden marriage, and the issue really was born illegitimate, though the validity of the marriage and the legitimacy of the issue could not be questioned in the country of domicile, by reason of the rules of the peculiar law, which made these matters cognizable in one tribunal only in that country. The marriage would be good in one sense, because it could not be set aside, and the issue would be legitimate in that sense, because there were no means provided by the English law to deprive them of the rights belonging to legitimate issue; but such marriages were all forbidden at the time of contracting them, all illegal, all capable of being set aside, as void *ab initio*, on account of their illegality; and the comity of nations cannot require them to be held valid in another country, where there exist no means of setting them aside."

LORD CHELMSFORD.

"The marriage of the parents of the respondent having
taken place prior to 1835, it is necessary to consider what
was the law of England, with respect to a marriage with a
deceased wife's sister before the Act of Parliament of that
year. I think it cannot properly be questioned that such
a marriage was void *ab initio*[1]. Now there was a well-
known maxim of our law, 'Quod ab initio non valet, in
tractu temporis non convalescit.' This rule would have
had its full force and operation in these marriages, if it
had not been for the interference of the Temporal Courts
with the proceedings of the Ecclesiastical Courts after the
death of one of the parents. This jurisdiction of the
Temporal Courts appears to have been exercised in favour
of the issue of the marriage, which they thus protected from
being bastardized, by preventing the Ecclesiastical Courts
from declaring a marriage to have been void, which had
been already dissolved by death. For it is to be observed,
as has been stated, that in these cases the Ecclesiastical
Courts pronounced no decree of divorce, but merely made
a declaration of the nullity of the marriage; and the
Temporal Courts only restrained the Ecclesiastical Courts
from making this declaration at a time when it could have
no practical effect upon the marriage itself, and when its
only operation would be to bastardize the issue. This is
not unimportant, as showing that the question of the
original validity of the marriage was not at all touched by
the Temporal Courts thus disabling the Ecclesiastical from
pronouncing a declaration respecting it. And that the
Temporal Courts by their interposition did not profess to

---

[1] Within a few weeks a Scottish tribunal has held the same marriage to
have been always illegal in Scotland, as being contrary to Scripture.

deal in any way with the validity of the marriage itself is
shown, by their leaving the Ecclesiastical Courts at liberty
to proceed to punish the surviving party for incest: a
power which, according to the opinion of Sir H. Jenner Fust,
continues even as to marriages protected by the Act of
1835. The respondent's condition therefore in England
was this,—he was the offspring of a marriage which was
incestuous and void, but of a marriage which by the course
of events had become irrevocable."

APPENDIX TO LETTER II.

*Extracts from a Letter of a Clergyman of South Carolina to
a Clergyman in England.*

" MARRIAGE with a deceased wife's sister has, I am sorry to
say, been growing to be customary among us. At the
beginning of our colonial history it was forbidden, of
course, under the English law then in force among us, as
in other parts of the British dominions; and in an Act
passed by the Legislature, in A.D. 1707, it was enjoined that
the 'Table of Prohibited Degrees' should be affixed
openly to every church-building as a guide to the people.
This Act has never been repealed, and it is pronounced by
high legal authority to be still binding. But it has been
going into desuetude of late years, only however since our
Independence. The first instance of its infringement was
somewhere about the year 1797, when a gentleman of
prominent social position in Charleston, and of eminent
services in the Revolutionary War, wishing to marry his
wife's sister, applied to Bishop Smith, the first of our
Bishops, to officiate. Bishop Smith, an Englishman by
birth and education, said he was not satisfied that it would
be right to comply with the gentleman's wishes, but
promised to consult some of his brethren elsewhere. He
did consult Bishop White, our first Bishop of English

ordination, and returning to Charleston consented to officiate.

"The marriage shocked the moral sense of the community very much, and the second wife, it was well known, was often troubled in her own mind about it. But the example nevertheless had weight, and became a precedent, followed at first by one and then another; the public mind each time revolting less and less, until such matches have become to be not only justified by many, but commended and preferred by some, and even advised by dying wives, one of whom, some years ago, joined the hands of her husband and her sister over her own dying bed, and gave them to each other! Whether this was because she saw they *would* marry, whether or no, may be a question. At any rate, now when a man's wife dies, the first idea of many if she leaves a sister is, that the widower will marry *her*. And he is almost regarded as wanting in due respect for her if he do not at least give her a chance of becoming her sister's successor. The plea on which these unions are recommended is, that the sister being already attached to the children of the previous marriage, and acquainted with the ways of the deceased, is better qualified and disposed than any one else could be to take her place and train up her offspring.

"But it is evident to those of us who are old enough to remember the state of things previously to this innovation, that it has brought about already a change for the worse. I can well recollect when ladies in the lifetimes of their husbands used to feel as if their brothers-in-law were their *own* brothers, and to treat them accordingly, in all the unreserve of domestic intercourse; when a brother-in-law, after an absence, would kiss his brother's wife 'in all purity' as his own sister, and she would confide in him without a thought of evil, or a feeling of embarrassment;

and when too, in case of a wife dying, her sister would
remain in charge of his family, or would remove to the
bereaved home, to live with the widower and take care of
his children as a thing of course, without a whisper of
slander, or any occasion for it; when the children, too,
knowing that their aunt could never be in any nearer
relation to them, loved and reverenced her, and confided in
her, and yielded readily a most wholesome influence to
her.

" But since such increased nearness of connexion has
been deemed not improper and even desirable, there has
grown up in families a perceptible and painful constraint,
the children learning to look with apprehension on their
mother's sisters, and the wives becoming jealous of their
influence with their husbands, while familiarities which
formerly were thought to be and really were innocent,
have come to possess a consciousness of evil tendency
which itself is of the nature of sin.

" I know of a wife whose health was gradually declining,
a woman of the world, with a husband as worldly as herself, and in their house was a young and attractive sister
of hers, between whom and her husband there had grown
up gradually a degree of affectionate intercourse which in
the days of the wife's health had been thought only natural. But as her end drew near it became on his part
more pointed, and drew to it her attention so agoniz-
ingly, that it became the one engrossing feeling of her
soul for the few last weeks of her life, exciting in her an
undisguised dread of what she foresaw would, as it did take
place, and so absorbed her as to shut out all thought of
religion and make her miserable to her very death.

" In another instance I knew of an excellent sister-in-law
who had been living with and watching over her sister's
children until the death of their mother, but who on that

mother's death would not remain another night in the widower's house, though he was left with children too young for him to take care of, and to whom she had become warmly attached, as they to her.

" I need not say that to my mind the matches referred to are very revolting. I never have officiated at one of them, and do not think I ever shall.

" But it is fair for me to add that others do not share the feelings I have thus expressed. Not only do laymen and laywomen thus married stand well in the communities wherein they live, but clergymen in good repute have formed such connexions, and bishops have officiated at them.

" Our Church in General Convention has never acted bindingly, i. e. by the joint action of the two Houses. But the House of Bishops in the year 1808 gave it as *their* opinion that the English Table of Prohibited Degrees is binding, and the two Houses appointed in 1838 a joint Committee to consider the subject, but the Report of that Committee was laid on the table in 1841, and attempts to take up the subject have been ineffectual, arising partly, I think, from apprehension of conflict with the civil authorities, but in great measure also from a feebleness of objection to, if not a positive approval of, marriages of the sort.

" Indeed, the public mind of our entire country seems to me to be alarmingly unsettled on this whole subject of marriage—the laws and usages in the different States being exceedingly diverse as to alike the formation and dissolution of the tie. In many of the States divorces and remarriages are shamelessly common, and for most trivial causes, and even pretences, and not a meeting takes place of Legislature, or Court, without numerous divorces being granted. Men meet in society sometimes with several women who have been successively their wives, and a story is told, I believe truly, of four couples in the same dance, each of whom by regular progress of law had exchanged wife or husband with one of the others, so that each man saw before him two women of whom one had been, as the other was then, his wife.

"That may be an extreme case, I will not vouch even for it being a fact; but I do know of persons in the best society in the town where they live, who do meet in that society those that once were joined to them in this closest of earthly ties, but who now are united to others, while they themselves in their turn have formed that tie anew, and yet associate familiarly with their discarded consorts.

"My best wishes attend you in your efforts to avert from your favoured isle such a state of things.

"If you make any public use of this letter, I request only that you do not mention my name, though if the accuracy of my statements be questioned, I shall be ready to substantiate them under my own signature if you desire it.

"I mention, as a perhaps not uninstructive instance of the unsteady movements of civil legislation when once the Bible is lost sight of, that in a neighbouring State, where divorce is allowed for almost any allegation, first cousins are forbidden to marry."

THE END.

www.ingramcontent.com/pod-product-compliance
Lightning Source LLC
Chambersburg PA
CBHW031448270326
41930CB00007B/909